THE LATIN QUARTER

Flavia Cosma

MadHat Press
Asheville, North Carolina

MadHat Press
MadHat Incorporated
PO Box 8364, Asheville, NC 28814

Copyright © 2015 Flavia Cosma
All rights reserved

Edited by Matt Loftin

The Library of Congress has assigned this edition a Control Number of 2015917114

ISBN 978-1-941196-21-2 (paperback)

Text by Flavia Cosma
Cover photograph by Miriam D. Goldfarb
Book and cover design by MadHat Press

www.MadHat-Press.com

First Printing

The Latin Quarter

Introduction to *The Latin Quarter*

The opening poem sets the stage for what transpires in Flavia Cosma's *The Latin Quarter*: "A heavy miasma brutally sweeps us / To other continents, other coasts," with the result being, "In our mind's eyes we see murky lakes, / Dark epidermis breathing desires, / Soft blue and orange skies, / Heart-breaking sadness, vast plains." As the poet absorbs her natural surroundings, the ultimate effect is "A bridge spanning the world, / This alien love / Consumes me wildly / With its boundless absence." While the image might be Wordsworthian, the book's primary pursuit, with its impossible longing for the union of souls, is Keatsian, for it is ultimately the creative imagination and nature's beauty that feeds the poet's hungry spirit. In short, the poems comprising *The Latin Quarter* represent a journey seeking fulfillment, a fulfillment that has as much to do with internal harmony as it does the union of two souls. Along the way the reader is swept beneath an undertow of brilliant imagery.

One's journey through *The Latin Quarter* is rewarded many times over by imagery that is startlingly beautiful. Cosma's cosmopolitan sensibility, enhanced no doubt by her translations from and into Romanian, from English, Spanish and French poets, reveals itself as she evokes various senses with her inventive imagery: "The sea rattles her bracelets, her bosom," "The fragrance of fresh hay / Invades us," "And the heavy bells of churches blackened with ages," "A duckling of lint floats on the waves," and "Your red eyes, / Your black eyes, / Your eyes, burnt worlds, / Hatched chicks—stars."

Cosma's poems are a language of the senses where concrete sensations express the abstract desire for harmony with self and the universe. Again, Keats: "O for a life of Sensations rather than of Thoughts!" Similar to Keats, Cosma's passion for extraordinary relationships, in one poem after another, inevitably forces her to succumb to the realization that a supreme union of souls is unlikely, if not impossible, and that spiritual harmony ultimately exists through her relationship with nature. One observes in Cosma that imagination is more suitable for her passion than the conventional world which is, alas, too much with her. Keats' "Heard melodies are sweet, but those unheard / Are sweeter;" is an apt summation. Occasionally, however, in these poems, a tenderness between souls does occur, as in "You, / As precious to me / As golden light gliding through stained glass panes," or, "The silvery alphabet of leaves, / The immaculate letter notched in stone, / The kiss—a deep impression / On a bare shoulder."

But, mostly, like Keats, lovers are ill-fated to chase their passions (around an urn) for eternity, doomed to remain apart, as Cosma laments time and time again that deep passions remain unfulfilled: "I embraced you blindly in my arms, / I melted you in fires / Unknown to me," then, "I presented you all the sky, stars, and moon, / I gave you absolutely / Everything you didn't need or want." Yet, even in lamentation there is tender beauty: "I dreamt of you yesterday and the day before too. / You came towards me, like then, / with a helpless smile, / And eyes ablaze with fever," which continues, "I waited with all my being to recognize your voice, / To sense at my nape your golden whisper stealing / Through the roots of my hair."

As *The Latin Quarter* evolves its fixation for romantic fulfillment, a number of poems through remarkable imagery reveal an intense bond with nature. Throughout the book, one is dazzled by brilliant terrestrial imagery. Cosma's cultivated sensibility captures in one remarkable image after another the incredible beauty and depth of feeling that nature provides for her expansive emotions: "Piously bearing crosses on their backs, / Spiders weave transparent strands / In the summer air," "The sea flings onto shore / Small stones, delicate bodies, / Shells shattered by storms, / Mottled eggs of guinea-hens," and,

> Plaintive,
> Your song
> Hums with the wind
> Through abandoned parks.
> The owl's screech
> Zigs and zags through this midnight,
> Backed by the panic-seized croaking
> Of stony toads.

While nature more often than not nourishes the poet's inwardness, Cosma occasionally seeks solace from the celestial realm. In "Journey Towards Evening" she invokes God, who could almost be a metaphor for advanced sensibility impatient with earthly blunderings:

> God, in His garden,
> Stamps His foot impatiently,
> Annoyed by so much turmoil,
> Bored by worldly torments,
> By this obstinate
> And unrequited longing.

And from "Flowers of Oblivion," God "returns to us, / Merciful, / His bag loaded with love remedies." While nature provides most of the spiritual comfort the poet desires, the final poem, "Divine Silence," unites terrestrial with celestial to produce the spiritual harmony that *The Latin Quarter* ultimately seeks:

> If it weren't for the startled bird
> Darting full speed over waters,
> Or for rain's tardy drops
> Beating drums on the damp planks,
> We would think that the Divine Harmony
> Descended to earth
> With the night.

Flavia Cosma

The Latin Quarter is an extraordinary book by a mature poet who has cultivated a unique lexicon. Flavia Cosma's imagery is inventive and immensely pleasing, even at times reminiscent of Lorca, Neruda, Ritsos and Mistral. Hers is a supreme accomplishment by a poet who is certain to increase her international readership with this book that has already been published in Romanian, Spanish, English, and French.

—Alan Britt, poet, essayist, university professor
Towson University, 2014

To all who
Like myself
Beg at Love's gates.

Table of Contents

Introduction — vii

Impossible Summer	1
The Bronze of Statues	2
Southern Continent	3
You, Keeper of Mysteries …	4
Disembodied Words	5
The Lamp's Flame	6
In the Cats' Shade	7
Invite	8
At the Close of the Day	9
Quicksands	10
Love in Contretemps	11
Out of the Great Sleep	12
This Prolonged Waiting …	13
Warmth	14
Bright Afternoons	15
The Paper	16
Finding You Again	17
Of Autumn	18
Your Shadow	19
The Great Transformation	20
The Soul of the Dead	21

Summer Tempests	22
Colorful Hills	23
The First of Boldness	24
Eternal Faith	25
The Ailing Grass	26
By Chance	27
Lotus Hands	28
Now Life, Now Love …	29
My Man, My Tree	30
Leaves' Sleep	31
The Twilights' Threshold	32
Presents	33
For Some Time	34
Steely Birds	35
If I Were to Speak to You …	36
Delirium	37
No	38
Transfiguration	39
On New Year's Eve	40
Plaza of Sighs	41
Blue Sleep	42
Journey Towards Evening	43
Uncertainty's Poison	44
A Young Sorrow	45
Flames at Dawn	46
Man's Iron Hand	47

The Apple of Love	48
Mad Desire	49
Flowers of Oblivion	50
Let's Divide the World …	51
Crucifixion	52
The Body's Mysteries	53
Prodigality	55
Ardent Prayer	56
On My Sky	57
Tongues of Fire	58
Shamelessness	59
Melancholy	60
The Slaughter's Place	61
In Passing	62
I Gathered It All …	63
Perpetual Motion	64
City's Arches	65
The Sign of The Cross	66
Sadness	67
Divine Silence	68
Acknowledgments	71
About the Author	73
Flavia Cosma—Selected Publications	75

Impossible Summer

Leavening, the air draws silt;
It smells like the city
Has moved to the shore
Of a lake—magic.

Gulls with ruffled feathers
Fall to sleep on hot asphalt;
A heavy miasma brutally sweeps us
To other continents, other coasts.
In our mind's eyes we see murky lakes,
Dark epidermis breathing desires,
Soft blue and orange skies,
Heartbreaking sadness, vast plains.

A bridge spanning the world,
This alien love
Consumes me wildly
With its boundless absence.

Flavia Cosma

The Bronze of Statues

Kissed on the lips, the bronze of statues
Transforms to gold;
The inert matter opens wide its eyes,
The soul breathes noisily,
A smoky trap, sweet breeze,
The air lustily seizes us.

Caressed on the breasts, the bronze of statues
Transforms to water,
Green water, blissful,
Covers the beloved's alabaster hands,
Floods his boundless heart
That beats and beats,
Stirs up oceans,
Runs with clouds,
Draws near.

Southern Continent

You remained the same as the mystery
Of your Southern continent,
Full of countries with sonorous names,
Overlapping on maps of the world.

Each of your words
Echoes strange tales
Of blood and wild dreams,
Each of your glances
Stands heavy with sin—
Alien to both you and me.

You walk, hesitate
On slippery roads,
While the ray of your eyes
—a bashful tentacle—
Withdraws slowly to
The protective, narrowed shell
Of a heavy, ancient,
Golden snail.

Flavia Cosma

You, Keeper of Mysteries …

You, keeper of mysteries,
How do you fill your hours, your thoughts?
Which paths do you wander now, my beloved?

Come on; recount everything to me in a whisper,
Tell me the truth, but only half—
Better not. Reveal
Just a fourth,
Or better still, so not to hurt,
Gently lie to me.

Spin a parable only for my use.
Tell me of a time that will never be
But never was, either,
Spin a deceptive bed-time fairy tale
Where you picked me from amid the stars
From arms of angels with slithery
Quicksilver bodies.

Disembodied Words

Wasted, fleshless words
Penetrate now and then
Through the room's walls;
Phantom-words, empty words
Wander through spaces,
Coming and going
Through famished dreams of the night.

Let us say good-bye now, my angel;
The time for leaving has caught us
And now outruns us.
It will haunt our next encounters,
Our first handshakes,
Our first exchanges of glances.

In rough, high-strung and vacillating sentences
We place the end before the beginning,
While love, foreseeing its fate,
Bitterly writhes.

Flavia Cosma

The Lamp's Flame

You have again left the lights
Turned on in the room,
                my beloved.

Plaintive,
Your song
Hums with the wind
Through abandoned parks.
The owl's screech
Zigs and zags through this midnight,
Backed by the panic-seized croaking
Of stony toads.

Only the dogs stay silent, pricking their large ears,
Sensing your thought—thief of hearts—
As you stealthily escalate
The six floors
To me.

But even then, were I to catch you unaware,
Stretched on the bed stark naked,
You wouldn't hesitate to say
That you returned only to extinguish
The lamp's flame.

In the Cats' Shade

Lascivious women, dyed-purple locks
And legs opened wide,
All-knowing,
Rest sprawled in the shade of cats,
Behind a dirty curtain.

An obscene smile twitches on their faces,
Uncovering teeth blackened by wormwood.
Stretched on used straw-mattresses,
Apathetic, they wait.

Not understanding, I let myself be carried
By these foreign, barbaric rhythms;
Half my soul
Hangs on the breeze's skirts
As coveted castles, with their grandiose gates,
Vanish in the distance.

Piously bearing crosses on their backs,
Spiders weave transparent strands
In the summer air.

In welcoming hollows,
The forest's pixies
—Diaphanous, superficial beings—
Wildly embrace each other,
Forever giggling,

Flavia Cosma

INVITE

Dwarfed mountains don't answer us anymore;
Trees with golden leaves
No longer shade only us;
Smooth, enveloping arms
Open powerlessly, heaving deep sighs;
Wounded hearts run and hide
Into foxes' reeking lairs;
Wedding bands remain benumbed
On ailing fingers before altars.

We were invited to sumptuous weddings,
From where, as by enchantment,
The groom was missing,
And the bride, her face painted red and black,
Begged on her knees
Before sacred images.

Dawns loom wide on encompassing seas.
Foreign vibrations lie in wait between
puzzled continents;
The sun ravages vast plains,
Its fires swallow us irrevocably,
Transforming us into dust, scattering us in wind,
An absolution, a sword in the sky

At the Close of the Day

In the honeyed light at the close of the day,
The birch trees are left naked and leafless,
Their white trunks shine under the light;
Pine trees shelter tender nests
—Their green, fragrant branches
Always ready to rescue—
The air smells like resin.

Neighbors kindle pyres of colored leaves;
Now and then a bird
Scolds me in flight;
Now and then the wind caresses me
With dreamy, ethereal fingers.

The sky and the mountains,
Silhouettes in the distance,
Possess absolute quietness,
Guard silently the heart's sorrows;
Your thoughts, a scented balm,
Knock again at my window
As if asking for forgiveness.

Flavia Cosma

Quicksands

We find ourselves again at the edge of the abyss,
dearest one,
In the same place from where, laughing,
 we once flung the moments
With great whirls.

We didn't imagine then
That days would turn to years,
And the years would become—as in a fairy-tale—
Old camels with strong claws.

It never even crossed our minds
That they would gnaw us, day by day,
with no respite,
Right to the core,
The sands moving under our feet.

Love in Contretemps

And we were taking turns
Pretending we don't care any more.

My turn comes
To discard silence
—A filthy rag—
At your feet.

It's my turn to wrap myself
In rippling, maleficent silks,
And laughingly rivet you
With chains of oblivion.

Poor love, always *en contretemps*;
Masks of contradictions proudly worn,
Futile gestures, mangled talk,
Withered eyelids noisily falling
Over the last word,
My word,
Yours.
Who knows whose?

Flavia Cosma

Out of the Great Sleep

The celestial orange
Tumbles noisily
On high stony steps.

Naked men hurl themselves into waves
A blond adolescent accompanies them cheerfully;
The sea rattles her bracelets, her bosom.

The transparence of simple things
Enchants me.

Young voices admire my garment.
I pull myself out of the old illnesses.

All is beautiful, beautiful indeed,
The wind whispers softly, bringing back to life from the abyss
Souls pregnant with the great sleep, and who,
Stretching lazily, in rapture again take up
The pink-colored dance
With sea and sky.

This Prolonged Waiting …

Oh! This prolonged waiting—
For your lips to whisper yes or no;
This fever—brimming with mysteries
Stolen straight from divine drawers,
And most of all
This impossible, tender miracle—
When disentangled from the claws of time,
We'll find ourselves free again.

We'll become intoxicated
From the moon's nectar;
We'll gather bright suns
Out of azure chasms;
Flocks of angels will merrily sing
Praise to our love.

Oh, Eternity!
Break from your chains
And secretly accomplish
This dreamy miracle!

Flavia Cosma

Warmth

The outline of your body
Appears like a specter on the threshold;
The warmth of your shoulder,
Thirsty, rummages in my bed;
Your fingers burrow beneath my pillows,
Searching for the illusive, precious grain,
Wanting to bring it back to earth,
In the world of these speechless plants,
Loving, creeping,
And above all
Perennial.

Bright Afternoons

Prisms of light
Dance through the branches.
The sun descends in a leisurely rhythm;
Perplexed clouds
Lie still on the vault.
An island of undulating grass smiles—
Its face mowed short;
The fragrance of fresh hay
Invades us;
Impatient hands shake with anticipation.

The hummingbird speaks to me of you;
Gently, the world's din entices me;
Lyrics transcend
From one dimension to another.
Saint John the Baptist
Quietly predicts
That man's soul
Will never die.

Flavia Cosma

The Paper

Pen in hand,
I sit at the table again,
Aimlessly scribbling across the paper.

Rushing into the room
Together with the bees
—Dizzy with the crisp shudder of morning—
Your name appears,
Dancing amid words,
Like a beautiful alabaster God.

Fiery letters pull me into their whirl,
And I don't recall when
Suddenly
I lost my whole body.
I remain just a voice, whispering to you,
Just a hand, transparently drawing
The miraculous outline of your eyes,
Your pallid brow,
Casting spells, imploring,
Loving you wildly
With all my yearning banished
To these immaculate
And blind sheets of paper.

Finding You Again

You,
As much unknown to me,
As falling raindrops on blue flowers,
You,
As necessary to me,
As the pure air, seeping into my lungs,
You,
As precious to me
As golden light gliding through stained-glass panes
Over hands clasped together in prayer,
Invoking peace, forgiveness,
And above all
Love.

You,
One day you will cross the sea and all the forests,
Weary, you'll stop in front of my gates,
And I'll welcome you, seized by a holy shiver,
My eyes filled with tears and my soul a nest

For belated, mellow loves.
Oh, beggar …

Flavia Cosma

Of Autumn

Flocks of leaves run down roads;
They are also afraid, more than I.
The wind blows in furiously from the lakes;
The leaves pause for a second
              and then,
Take to their heels in a contrary direction,
Seized by sudden amnesia.

It rains a rusty whirlwind
Over quiet dogs,
Over rotten benches.
Snarling robots stand frozen in bestiaries;
Masked children scour the streets
In search of dreams once lost,
In a virtual childhood.

Your Shadow

All the bodies in the world
Don't mean to me
Nearly as much as your shadow.

All the heart's uprisings
Along the length and width
Of blind energetic fields,
Don't throb like the pulse of your thought,
Always awake, keeping vigil in the night,
With its scorched, purple ray.

Wait for me dearest one,
I'll come back to you soon,
I'll break the bottles, the mirrors, the china,
And the heavy bells of churches blackened with ages.

Then I'll dare know you
As you really are.
You'll know me
As I am.

Flavia Cosma

The Great Transformation

In situations like this,
The line between life and death
Grows misty, disappears.

Under winter's purple sky
The real world becomes a fairy-tale;
Snowflakes fall, full of humid astonishment,
Accompanying the vapid ticking of the clock,
Through torturous waiting hours.

My yearning after you, a hostile shadow,
Covers the skyline, intensifies,
The ice melts in narrow strips,
The faltering gait sinks into slush,
Alien blood runs in torrents down our cheeks,
Mirrors uncover otherworldly beings,
Shards of self await
A great transformation.

The Soul of the Dead

A duckling of lint floats on waves;
My grandmother's soul waits for me in the cemetery.
Today I will go to wake once more
Her old bones,
In the dripping shade of small candles,
And of peaceful, leafy chestnut-trees.

Once a year,
Her memory carries me back to our great love,
To our great understanding,
And to the sorrow of being torn from her—
Always present in my mind.

Who would have thought that on days like these,
Grandmother would have to share
The warmth in my heart
With you, foreigner?

Flavia Cosma

Summer Tempests

The end knocks insistently at the door,
Pulling along both misery and nausea;
Everything dissipates
As if it were
Just useless child's play,

A sand castle erected bit by bit
Only in the delirious fevers
Of my mind.

Thus our grounds
Don't overlap any more.
Did they ever?

The air that we once drank so greedily,
Isn't the same today,
It doesn't exhilarate us anymore.

So you remain there
While I stay here;
You have wisely built for yourself
Dams against violent storms,
While I stagger, a frightened bough,
 Into the whirlwind
Of summer tempests.

Colorful Hills

The colors close upon me again
With their soft gait of flesh, of flower,
Passions appear woven into carpets
—Lavender-gold and pink-violet—
Like the great sunsets
Covering hills over-ripe with longing
In radiant mantles.

Heat scorches all in its big furnaces,
Wholly transforming
The Templars' shadows walking through ruins,
Green and blue fields,
And the forest's leaves—red fans—
Into silvery smoke, into ashes of oblivion.

A late rain licks dried river-beds,
Touching in passing your absent ankles,
With voluptuous wings
Of emerald and sun.

Flavia Cosma

The First of Boldness

Imperfection hides from sight
Under cover of boiling waters;
Lakes carrying priceless treasures
Spring steaming from mineral soils.

Curative waters, quietly bubbling,
Fill to the brim blue swimming pools.
People submerge themselves beneath deceptive waves,
The lie transformed into a white cat,
Slips amidst the patients drowsy with heat,
With the boldness of first youth.

Eternal Faith

And what is family
But a bed
Where you don't want to lie down and sleep,
Next to a woman you once loved,
To whom you pledged in life's morning,
Before the altars,
Eternal love.
An artificial reality
Made so day after day,
Sweet words, transformed into sweat,
High stony walls
Behind which red roses
Become bunches of thorns,
And on the outside of these silent gates,
Enticing, vast distances
Through which you won't be allowed
To ever roam.

Flavia Cosma

The Ailing Grass

Hemmed
With yellow leaflets fallen from the sky,
The ailing grass awaits
Both winter and death.

You ought to know, my beloved,
Autumn is here already.
The signs are heavy; nothing seems beautiful anymore,
Neither the tears, nor the flower,
Nor the picture on the wall.

All things sift through the sieve of profound sleep;
Stifling dreams shatter in a cold sweat;
Life's threads lie tangled, torn,
Fruits swollen with late mists rain down;
Rats with long rabbit ears
Hide under our armpits, in our hair,
And a cat's eyes,
Seized by a great disappointment
Stagger on sea waves
Meowing.

The paper virgin
Locks herself in her room,
Weeping,
Cursing.

By Chance

If by chance I unlocked the door,
And you were there, lying on the bed,
Watching the small screen,
I would implore you to remain still,
As if I'd never entered your life,
As if I wouldn't carry, as a sad banner,
Your heart within mine,
The paper heart that you present and promise me,
Every time you sense
That the thread of life
Has abandoned me.

Flavia Cosma

Lotus Hands

From lotus hands stretched on waters
A big uproar reaches up to us,
Which, joined with the ravens' screech,
Tears the nocturnal equilibrium.

A shrill noise fills the vault;
The nothingness is full, can't accommodate
Even a whisper.
There is nothing else of value
For us to say or add.

Birds and angels
Shamefaced, withdraw into barns
And cry without tears.

Now Life, Now Love …

Life diminishes until
It becomes no more than
A mathematical symbol,
A dot on the paths of the sky,
A possibility on the horizon.

While love,
Grows impetuously, careless of the passing of time,
A foamy wave, a sea torn from the sea,
Heavenly flood,
Perpetual calling,
Tiger Royal, roaring,
Awaiting.

Flavia Cosma

My Man, My Tree

Hold me by the hand
Man-tree, tree-man,
As though protecting a lost child
Protect me.

Let me drink quickly
From your painted palms,
Painted green, painted red,
Painted in spring colors.
Let me drink your sweet wine,
              your wormwood wine,
Your happy tears,
Your bitter tears.

Man-tree, tree-man,
Weave me tightly
Within the magic threads of your roots.
Bury my words and my fear
In your wholesome silences.

The sleepy lullaby,
The gentle lullaby,
Let it softly heal
Both my heart and my wings.

Leaves' Sleep

Clay leaves,
Slowly rot on dark branches,
Millions of leaves, glide over the world,
On wind's soft wings,
Carpets of leaves,
—Crimson tears—
Rustle under the sad steps
Of great, unfulfilled loves;

In the autumn's sleep someone finds you
Sitting on an old bench, always waiting.
Leaves embrace you in their protective arms,
Infinite longings turn back at sunset,
Touching your stony soul
With golden autumn's fingers.

Perhaps,
Before the night fall
The long-predicted fate will come true;
Perhaps,
On slippery paths,
In a fairy-dream
Again I'll be with you.

Flavia Cosma

The Twilight's Threshold

A bunch of purple-pink roses
Grow, withering slowly, in a vase.

Watching them, I think
That they were cut last night in the garden,
By a man crossing anxiously
Over twilight's threshold,
And then presented, tremulously,
To some eyes twined in their turn
With the nightfall

The roses are wondering in agony—
Why do two people on the thresholds
Dare offer each other flowers;
What significances
Do these ephemeral emanations
Of bashful gentility
Still have for them?

Presents

I never looked at you
With the absent eye of occasional friendship.
I didn't study you
As a dead spider
In a terrarium.
I didn't have time to pause
At your eyes reddened by insomnia,
Or at your lips tumescent
With hidden vices.

I embraced you blindly in my arms,
I melted you in fires
Unknown to me,
I changed you,
And resurrected you in pain,
I transformed you to an angel
With a silvery mantle,
I presented you all the sky, stars, and moon,
I gave you absolutely
Everything you didn't need or want.

Flavia Cosma

For Some Time

The sky welcomes us again
In its arms, white branches thrown open.
Flames—young girls—spring up from the walls,
Butterflies painted with yellow eyes on wings
Writhe in the mud,
With a raspy voice, the echo
Calls you by name.

For some time
All we own await us on the other side,
We must hurry because today
We still have to learn together
The silvery alphabet of leaves,
The immaculate letter notched in stone,
The kiss—a deep impression
On a bare shoulder.

Steely Birds

The sky hums with steely birds;
Walking sticks beat flagstones in time.
The temple's weary heart throbs;
Day swims out of night's rain gutters.

I am still thinking of the time,
This much too brief time
Left to me—
Which unravels like a dried sponge
Amid your nice words.

I linger in my sleep,
In a dream, rummaging
Through the laced pockets on my night gown,
Searching for the address
Where I should have met
The greatest of loves.

Flavia Cosma

If I Were to Speak to You …

If I were to speak to you,
And if you were to listen,
I would tell you of an opaque silence
That lately surrounds me;
About the toil of my feeble body
Dreaming of your hands,
And about all of those from the other side,
Who wait, just as hungry,
Drawing nearer and nearer to the border,
Stretching their paper faces
Night after night by the side of my bed,
Climbing,
Nestling right here on my pillow,
Into the very memory of you.

Delirium

I dreamt of you yesterday and the day before, too.
You came towards me, like then,
                          with a helpless smile,
And eyes ablaze with fever.
I waited with all my being to recognize your voice,
To sense at my nape your golden whisper stealing
Through the roots of my hair,
Wanting you with a passion conceived in delirium.
And you
Ended by transforming yourself
First into a trembling, undulating snake,
Then into a dog-cat,
Sorrowfully fawning
At my feet.

No

It's not the great blue I fear,
I am not hungry for crystal waters.

I am hungry for you,
It's you I'm afraid of.

Diminutive stars fall splashing on hot sands.
Shards of thought hurriedly traverse the seas;
Ideas skip over green and blue crests,
To catch me and strike angrily
Over my bare feet.

I didn't tell you until now,
But I ran away from home.
I don't know why or since when;
I've gotten stranded here on these slippery rocks,
Where if I were to incline my ear to the waves
I could hear you breathing.

Keep me by your left side;
I am just an angel's feather,
Inebriated on a salted, sharp wind,
Which, even if it reaches us only as a moan,
Doesn't compare with anything
Except the reckless thirst
In my heart.

Transfiguration

Windowpanes melt to mirrors;
The mirrors fuse into waves,
Changing over time
To windowpanes.

Mysteries deepen into night;
A perpetual tide becomes a footbridge
Between this world and a fairy tale.

Dreams and nightmares lie heavy on our chests.
A band of phantoms hurriedly surrounds us,
Chasing us with strange gestures from one sleep
                      to another;
Something is missing, yet here seems to be everything,
But awake, we do not remember;
We are driven by alien impulses
As if somebody
Has programmed us in advance.

Threads of quiet draw us always back
Toward dear graves,
And amid startled candles flickering
We rediscover the peace of ancient rooms,
The calmness of today, and even, sometimes,
The meaning of tomorrow.

Flavia Cosma

On New Year's Eve

It snows
A fresh coat of snow,
Over the seasons' greetings;
Snows solemnly
Over astonished beings
Caught blindly in love's fishing nets.

Under fluffy carpets of snow,
Wicked, disheveled fairies desecrate
Convents widowed of grace;
Tears bide their time—phosphorescent flowers
On stony faces.

The pallid sun, emptied of strength,
Gathers its brow in its palms;
A sticky, frozen mist,
Takes the place
Of mothers and fathers for us.

Plaza of Sighs

The sun emerges once more from the clouds.
The day shows itself, beautiful and whole.
Yet, who can predict it all?
I remain here in the plaza of sighs,
Waiting still, as you left me,
With my hands outstretched,
And your image in my mind.

New friends spring from the ground;
Unknown people invite me to dinner.
I'm thirsty for change, and how I wish
To cross past the grandiose gates,
But I'm so afraid that if I did
I would lose you forever.

Flavia Cosma

Blue Sleep

In my outstretched hands I carry
The horizon, absence,
A cherished image hidden in mists.

My knees bend
Under thousands of ephemeral kilograms,
An ethereal, cruel illusion
Weighs on me more and more heavily.

I sink into the sand and the stone;
Oval forms leave prints
Lengthwise on my body,
The day's toil disappears into powder of clouds;
I abandon myself to foaming shores,
And playful waves try to pull me on high seas
Promising me deep sleep—
Gentle and blue beyond words.

Journey Towards Evening

I arrive at sleep's customs
My eyes half open,
My heart a gate forgotten unlocked,
A bitter lump impetuously growing
In my blood and in my throat.

Today everything remains the same,
Warm, salt tears
Drift eyelid to pillow,
My soul fidgets, uneasy.

Behind large, rusty gratings,
Bands of anxieties hold council.

God, in His garden,
Stamps His foot impatiently,
Annoyed by so much turmoil,
Bored by worldly torments,
By this obstinate
And unrequited longing.

Flavia Cosma

Uncertainty's Poison

Modest snows piously enwrap
Bald, stout mountains;
Climbing roses stretch on neighboring fences;
Dwarfed haystacks confine in their humid cores
The sweet smell of a summer that passes;
A sharp green invades the forest;
Undulating, soft tentacles reach for us
Spattered to the elbows with the same crimson questions;

White corollas quaff greedily
Devout poison of doubts—
The same that has prowled around us
For now more than a year.

A Young Sorrow

Trying to understand this rabid passion,
I dream of new, unearthly loves;

Life withdraws on tiptoes with all that's hers,
The world fills up in turn
With old melancholies and new refrains.

Occurrences—
Seen or unseen,
Proper or improper,
Arrange themselves in silky folds.
Your hands,
Your somber eyes
Shining strangely through nights with low moons,
Your words, dulled stony knives,
Settle as masters in my house, at my table;

Overwhelmed by so much grief,
This young sorrow hurls its mantle to the ground
And, humming, disappears,
Leaving me more orphaned;
While I,
Stand at the window
Whiter by the mercy of years
In perpetual winter.

Flavia Cosma

Flames at Dawn

Like the sun's rays piercing me at dawn,
Your body comes back to mind
Consumes me head to toe,
Radiates to my vaults
—As incandescent fountains—
Its sweet and bitter mystery.

Your imaginary embrace
Transforms me to a pyre,
And I burn brightly with rainbow-flames,
While the pines, the forest's sages,
Caress me with thorny fingers.

Life goes on in primeval ways,
The wind breathes gently, encircling
The whirl of the heart and other painful miracles,
With its mantle, a light melody
That descends slowly from a blue chasm.

Man's Iron Hand

The hills soften under man's iron hand.
Their green spines groan under the weight.
Their curled and wiry hair teems with birds
Mating secretly
In the fragrant shade of acacias.

Diaphanous omens and dead dragonflies,
Float on twilight waters.
A sad murmur recalls the time,
The first and the last,
That you grasped me in your arms,
Shuddering and hiding
Even from yourself.

Fear leaped from your knees straight to my heart,
Left me wordless, blue poison on my lips,
As our roads trickled in opposite directions,
Under the suffocating heat
Of that southern December.

Flavia Cosma

The Apple of Love

Take a bite please, from this apple!
Once,
I tasted this very one in my turn.
Maybe I should have waited,
For us to have it together
Embracing in crisp linens
That savor of chamomile flowers.

It's not my fault
That I came to this world before you;
It's not your fault
You were born so late.
We can choose neither the hour nor the instant.
Fate wanted this, my dearest.

And yet, I beg, I implore,
Bite just once
Into this apple!
Get drunk
On the rounded dreams.
Its seeds will surely thrive
In your gardens too.

Mad Desire

Today I came back to the seashore
But I didn't look for you.
The rain had washed the beach, scattered the sightseers;
A mist stirred the skyline playfully,
And small waves cheerfully caressed
My toes, my ankles, my life.

Tenderly the sea sang ...

The house stays locked, empty on the hillock;
Two old men walk slowly on the quay;
Miasmas of rotting algae
Fill me heavily, smoothly entice me
To let myself be seized by a mad desire
To lie down on these waters
And slowly drift away.

Flavia Cosma

Flowers of Oblivion

When we lose what was most dear to us,
When Eternity bereaves us and leaves us
Arms empty, groping blindly,
God returns to us,
Merciful,
His bag loaded with love remedies.

All the possibilities wait for us
To welcome them back home,
They wait smiling by the gates
Like beautifully adorned brides
Fragrant with oblivion's flowers.

Let's Divide the World ...

Ugly, feathered apparitions,
Heaps of memories blackened by time,
Shrieking crows rushing into void,
Nefarious prophecies frightening
Those timid shadows of evening.

Yet not everything was deadly;
There were lights too,
Mantles of soft gold, embroidered over sleepless nights,
Sweet-scented flowers, a fool's happiness,
A smiling child braving his destiny,
Tranquil, colorful sunsets,
And the dog in the garden,
Dutifully sleeping
In the shade of yellow flowers.

Let's divide the world into halves:
You take what's embodied in pairs,
Leave for me a solitary soul,
A blade of grass, humid shores,
And free, rebellious waves;
Allow me a Lebanese cedar,
Stubbornly tethered to rocks,
Orphaned stars and the moon
—A rusty scythe—
Always weeping after the sun
On the sky's vault.

CRUCIFIXION

Crucified, I lie on steely wings;
Unwilling, I glide beside a miraculous bird.

The clouds fawn, obedient at my feet,
Nothingness cautiously pricks up its ears.

Toward sunrise I glide,
While all my being resists,
And your thought—a magnet—
draws me back
To the southern pole,
To that place
Where,
Under a leaden sun,
The summer's ardent fever froze
In our hearts—overwhelmed, astonished.

The Body's Mysteries

Wings carry me lightly
To places where
Aroused blue tempests whirl.

                      Here, explosions occur—
Heavenly bodies made of cold, drenched gold
Give birth in agony to stars.

A hand writes the Divine Will
With ink from the depths.

Yet something has changed at the body's gates:
On the pavement, in the street, drunks skirmish;
The uproar attracts the curious—
The Earth's drumbeats writhe in our ears,
closer and closer.

Rarely do I glance
Towards the gates of the soul,
The very place where, once
Peace, an empress, reigned,
Young angels, laughing impishly,
Caroused with the lint of clouds.

The falling snow
Buried them alive;
Not a single prayer comes down from Heaven anymore.
The vaults don't ring with song.

Flavia Cosma

Crouched in a corner,
The guard stays alone,
Mute and ready to scuttle away.

Prodigality

My gentle snare, my dearest one,
I recognize myself in your desires
To a point—

I follow obediently your path
To the crossroads.

Striding along afterward, I outrun you
Blazing in dancing flames, blue swords,
Scatter myself across the horizon,
At sunset

—As, frightened,
You lock yourself in your hard ways,
In a grotto of ice.

Flavia Cosma

Ardent Prayer

Be condescending, Father!
Lower upon me your steely eyes.
Take me in your mighty arms,
Reward my fervor since I fulfilled
Your difficult commandments—
Give me a sign, grant me a life,
Quench my thirst, chase away my sorrow,
Admit me as a guest at your lavish banquets!
Resurrect me with your rays, O, Master!
Transform me and let me be
As I was at the start,
A willow branch, growing from your body,
A wandering smile
Seeking completion.

On My Sky

You forgot
Your wings
In my sky,
       angel,

You forgot your eyes
At my shores.
They lie in wait for me
Half buried in sand,
Your red eyes,
Your black eyes,
Your eyes, burnt worlds,
Hatched chicks—stars.

Your passion mounts in waves,
Your heart calls out to mine,
Bolts shatter, roaring,
Mists glitter, cloth spread over waters.

Come back and take me with you, dearest one,
Let's climb the blue hill hand in hand,
To the spot where weakling kittens
Are born over and over
From your memory.

Flavia Cosma

Tongues of Fire

Families of glossy snakes
Swarm inside me;
Mother-snakes and slithery hatchlings;
"Our time has come," they hiss.
Rivers overflow their banks,
Bridges tumble to the ground,
Tongues of fire clean my heart of words,
Good, bad, plain, indifferent;
My blood lets itself be devoured
By thousands of leeches.

I steal out of military churches—
Hot furnaces writhe in my womb.
It doesn't make sense to plead for mercy anymore,
Pious parents forgot me here,
And softly they dissolve on the vault.

Toads mate in flight with wooden blackbirds,
Leap through the air, roaring,
The same as yesterday.

Shamelessness

You stay naked under the moonbeam;
I am also naked, but alas, how far away!
Laughing, the waves kidnap you to sea,
Empty, my room whimpers,
The mirror's eyes hide, guilty,
Under visceral linens.

Sweet words long to catch me;
I wait at the window for your return,
For you to softly lay me on this scented shroud
Woven from stars' hair and clay.

Melancholy

The snow spreads, chaste,
Over the melancholy of yesterday.
It snows immaculately over your ardent words,
Heated red-hot to exasperation,
In the furnaces of your Southern continent,
Where cold means hot,
And sweet means bitter,
Or vice versa.

Unloved lovers crowd at madhouse gates,
A crumpled love squats blackened on a fence;
Big, watery flakes cover its eyes,
And the tears that fancied themselves
All alone in the world
Fall in waves of slanting snow
From the sky,
Together with angels.

The Slaughter's Place

Then who was the one to stab the horizon?
The little stars wonder,
And the moon whimpers, half hidden under covers.
Curious ships draw cautiously near
The slaughter's place.

I withdraw behind curtains—
I find it difficult to watch
The results of your cruelty.

Fragrant oils caress my face
As an empress dead much too soon;
The warmth of a passing day lazes between linens.

There is no way for you to ever come back—
You can't make the binding leap into void,
And as a necessary gesture,

Embark on the path of return.

Flavia Cosma

In Passing

Shriveled, a man's body
Slowly withers.
With a determined step,
His time draws near to an end.
A large cemetery, a deep grave,
Lies patiently in wait.

Only the heart's flower pines
For another flower
With whom to pair its thoughts—
Flames are extinguished
In a futile quest.

People decide as living persons do—
They would demolish ancient crypts
Where sleep the ones whose descendants also died,
They would build instead public gardens,
Children's playing fields,
Benches where young lovers
Would whisper to each other sweet nothings—
Not even imagining
That the dead will hunt them with no respite,
Wanting to make whole for the Last Judgment,
Their fleshless fingers
And their worn-out, aching limbs.

The Latin Quarter

I Gathered It All …

I gathered it all in pairs:
Two water-glasses, two tablespoons,
Two snowy, fluffy pillows,
Two soup plates, two dinner dishes,
Crystal goblets, Sèvres porcelains,
—Always two of everything.

I filled up cupboards, pantries, days,
Carefully, bashfully,
Year after year, instant to instant,
I lived with twin images in mind,
I breathed two silences, I cried two tears,
                —one for you—

I adored symmetry …

Just one thing is missing—
You,
The one who should have turned up at dawn,
When the pale moon roused the lark
Gently from sleep.

Flavia Cosma

Perpetual Motion

The sea flings onto shore
Small stones, delicate bodies,
Shells shattered by storms,
Mottled eggs of guinea-hens,
The yellow sunset,
Imitations of wounded hearts,
And so much more …

Howling waves paw the sand;
Your shadow runs to the distance;
You don't even notice
How fast you are fading away,
And leaving all behind.

City's Arches

The city's arches,
Twist diaphanously over deep rivers.

You're right—they say—but only from a moral perch,
Legally you lost long ago
All contests,
All opportunities,
Hope itself.

You are naked, facing
The world and time.

Flavia Cosma

The Sign of The Cross

The sign of the cross
Softly covers
All others.

A hand glides smoothly over foreheads, over thoughts,
Devout fingers caress
Now the right shoulder,
Now the left.

Lowering its ray over my body,
The Holy Spirit dares to remind me savagely
Of you,
Of your cramped gesture, stopped
Just when it was about to solve
Our dilemmas.

Sadness

Rest your thoughts on my bosom, my beloved,
Stay silent and listen to the tumult of the flesh
Rising to the surface from a great abyss.

Pay attention to this infant left blind forever—
Memorize his whispers, his butterflies,
Cut down before soaring.

Love me as I am
Both barren and sorrowful,
For only then would you be able
To understand what was the thing
That was lost
In the void between us.

DIVINE SILENCE

On the green surface of the deep river,
Leaves float
in ordered rows.
Now and then a cat
Mumbles in sleep;
Unachieved desires are wasted in our thoughts.

Words in packs—round hieroglyphs—
Entirely at ease with their fate,
Slacken their pace solemnly
As they pass beneath bridges.

If it weren't for the cars' rumble,
Wounding the peace of twilight,
If it weren't for the startled bird
Darting full speed over waters,
Or for rain's tardy drops
Beating drums on the damp planks,
We would think that the Divine Harmony
Descended to earth
With the night.

Acknowledgments:

"Man's Iron Hand" appeared in *Hinchas de Poesia*, 2012.

"Impossible Summer" appeared in *Crannóg Magazine* 24, Ireland, 2012.

"The Ailing Grass," "The Body's Mysteries" and "Let's Divide the World" appeared in *Truck*, January 2013.

"Clay Leaves," "Delirium" and "Transfiguration" appeared in *Levure Littéraire* 7, 2013.

"Love in Contretemps," Bright Afternoons" and "For Some Time" appeared in *La Otra—Revista de Poesia*, Mexico, June 2013.

"Perpetual Motion," "The Bronze of Statues," "The Sign of The Cross," "Out of the Great Sleep" and "For Some Time" appeared in *Levure Littéraire* 9, 2014.

"Fleshless Words," "You, Keeper of Mysteries," "Presents," "Melancholy," and "Divine Silence" appeared in *Muddy River Poetry Review*.

"I Gathered it All …" appeared in *Poetic Diversity*.

About the Author

Flavia Cosma is an award-winning Romanian-born Canadian poet, author and translator. She has a Master's degree in Electrical Engineering from the Polytechnic Institute of Bucharest. Later she studied Drama at the Community School of Arts—Bucharest, Romania. She is also an award-winning independent television documentary producer, director, and writer, and has published twenty-seven books of poetry, a novel, a travel memoir and five books for children. Her work has been represented in numerous anthologies in various countries and languages, and her book *47 Poems* (Texas Tech University Press) received the ALTA Richard Wilbur Poetry in Translation Prize.

Cosma was nominated three times for the Pushcart Prize with poems from *Leaves of a Diary* (2006), *The Season of Love* (2008) and *Thus Spoke the Sea* (2008).

Flavia Cosma was awarded Third Prize in the 2007 John Dryden Translation Competition, for co-translating *In The Arms of The Father*, poems by Flavia Cosma (British Comparative Literature Association & British Literary Translation Centre)

Cosma's *Songs at the Aegean Sea* made the Short List in the Canadian Aid Literary Awards Contest, Dec. 2007. Her translation into Romanian of *Burning Poems* by George Elliott Clarke was published in Romania in 2006. Her translation from Spanish into Romanian of work by the Argentinean poet Luis Raul Calvo was published in 2009 under the title *Nimic Pentru Aici, Nimic Pentru Dincolo*. Her translation into Romanian of work by the USA poet Gloria Mindock was published in 2010 under the title *La Porțile Raiului*. Her translation into English of *Profane Uncertainties* by the Argentinean poet Luis Raul Calvo was published by Cervena Barva Press in 2010. Her translation into Romanian of *Lettres à Saïda* by the French poet Denis Emorine was published in Romania under the title *Scrisori pentru Saïda* in 2012.

Her translation into Romanian of work by the Peruvian poet Jose Guillermo Vargas was published in 2012 under the title *Oboseala centaurului/El cansacio del centauro*. Flavia translated *Manhattan Song—cinci poeme occidentale* (Ars Longa, 2013), by Luis Benitez, Buenos Aires, Argentina, and *Sans nom/Fără nume* (Ars Longa, 2013), by Patricia Tenorio, Recife, Brasil.

Cosma's poetry book *Leaves of a Diary* was studied at the University of Toronto E. J. Pratt Canadian Literature during the school year 2007–2008. Her poetry book, *Thus Spoke the Sea*, was taught during the spring 2014 semester by Professor Alan Britt at Towson University, Baltimore, Maryland, USA.

Flavia Cosma received the Title of Excellence for outstanding contribution in the promotion and enrichment of the Romanian culture within the European region and throughout the world, awarded by The International Festival "Lucian Blaga," XXIX edition, Sebeș-Alba, Romania, 2009

Flavia was decorated with the Golden Medal and was appointed Honorary Member by the Casa del Poeta Peruano, Lima, Peru, 2010, for her poetry and her work as an international cultural promoter.

Flavia Cosma is the Director of the International Writers' and Artists' Residence at Val-David, Quebec, Canada (www.flaviacosma.com/Val_David.html), and the Director of the Biannual International Festivals at Val-David.

Flavia Cosma is the International Editor for Červená Barva Press, Somerville, MA, USA

Flavia Cosma: **http://www.flaviacosma.com**

FLAVIA COSMA—AWARDS

—*47 Poems* (Texas Tech University Press, 1992), won the prestigious ALTA Richard Wilbur Poetry in Translation Prize.

—*Romania, A Country at the Crossroads*, a TV documentary by Flavia Cosma, won the Canadian Scene National Award (1992).

—Primer Premio—Paz en el Mundo Competition 2005, Bilingual Writers MCA, Buenos Aires, Argentina, for the poem "The Season of Love."

—Flavia Cosma was nominated three times for the Pushcart Prize with poems from *Leaves of a Diary* (2006), *The Season of Love* (2008) and *Thus Spoke the Sea* (2008).

—Honorable Mention Award from The Ontario Poetry Society—Open Heart Competition 2007, for the poem "Cradle-Song."

—Third Prize in the 2007 John Dryden Translation Competition, for co-translating *In The Arms of The Father*, poems by Flavia Cosma (British Comparative Literature Association & British Literary Translation Centre).

—Flavia Cosma's *Songs at the Aegean Sea* made the Short List in the Canadian Aid Literary Awards Contest, Dec. 2007.

—Cosma was listed as a finalist in the 6° Certamen Internacional de Poesia "La lectora impaciente", Gandia-Valencia, Spain, 2008, with her poems "Dance" (Danza), "You're not a Tiger" (No se es un tigro), "Don't Speak" (No hables) and "Resurrection" (Resurreccion)

—Flavia Cosma received the Title of Excellence for outstanding contribution in the promotion and enrichment of the Romanian culture within the European region and throughout the world, awarded by The International Festival "Lucian Blaga", XXIX edition, Sebeş-Alba, Romania, 2009

—Flavia Cosma received the title of Honorary Member of Casa del Poeta Peruana and was decorated with The Golden Medal at the III International Poetry Festival in Huari, Peru, September 2010, for her poetry and her work as an international cultural promoter.

Selected Publications—English

ON PATHS KNOWN TO NO ONE, Červená Barva Press, 2012
POSTCARDS FROM RHODES, Variety Crossing Press, 2010
MOONLIGHT FAIRY TALES, In Our Own Words Inc. Press, 2009
THUS SPOKE THE SEA, KCLF-21 Press, 2008
THE SEASON OF LOVE, Červená Barva Press, 2008
A COUNTRY OF ONE, www.brindin.com 2007
THE ADVENTURES OF TOMMY TEDDY BEAR AND ALEX LITTLE BUNNY, Korean-Canadian Literary Forum-21 Press, 2007
GOTHIC CALLIGRAPHY, Červená Barva Press, 2007
LEAVES OF A DIARY, Korean-Canadian Literary Forum-21 Press, 2006.
FATA MORGANA, Edwin Mellen Press, 2003
WORMWOOD WINE, Edwin Mellen Press, 2001, 2004
THE FIRE THAT BURNS US, Singular Speech Press, 1996
47 POEMS, Texas Tech University Press,1992 (Richard Wilburn ALTA Prize for translation)
FAIRY TALES, Canadian Stage and Arts, 1990

Selected Publications—French

Griffures sur le miroir, Editions du Cygne, Paris, France, 2015
Quartier latin, Edition du Cygne, Paris, France, 2014.
Le corps de la lune, Editions du Cygne, Paris, France, 2014
Le miel trouble du matin, L'Harmattan, Paris, France, 2012

Selected Publications—Spanish

ARAÑAZOS SOBRE LA FAZ DEL ESPEJO, Editorial Torremozas, Madrid, España, 2015
EL CUERPO DE LA LUNA, Editorial Maribelina, Lima, Perú, 2013
EL BARRIO LATINO, Editorial Maribelina, Lima, Perú, 2012
HOJAS DE DIARIO, Editorial Maribelina, Lima, Perú, 2011
PLUMAS DE ANGELES, Editorial Dunken, Buenos Aires, Argentina, 2008

Selected Publications—Romanian

SĂLBĂTICIUNI ȘI UMBRE, Editura Ars Longa, 2015
LINIȘTE DIVINĂ, (ediție bilingvă Româno/Albaneză), Amanda Edit Verlag, Bucharest, 2015
ZGÂRIETURI PE FAȚA OGLINZII, Editura Ars Longa, 2013
TRUPUL LUNII, Editura Ars Longa, 2012
PE CĂI DE NIMENI ȘTIUTE, Editura Ars Longa, 2011
FOCUL CE NE ARDE, Ars Longa Press, 2011
CARTIERUL LATIN, Ars Longa Press, 2011
POVEȘTI SUB CLAR DE LUNĂ/ CONTES DE FÉES, (édition bilingue Romanian/French), Ars Longa Press, 2009
NEANT BINEVOITOR, Semne Press, 2007
CÂNTECE LA MAREA EGEE, Editura Ars Longa, 2007
TEATRU PENTRU COPII MICI ȘI MARI, Familia Press 2007
IN BRAȚELE TATĂLUI, Cogito Press, 2006
RHODOS SAU RHODES SAU RODI, Jurnal Sentimental, Limes Press, 2005
JURNAL, CogitoPress, 2004
AMAR DE PRIMĂVARĂ, România Libera Press, 2003
CINĂ CU DEMONI, Eminescu Press 1999
PĂSĂRI ȘI ALTE VISE, Eminescu Press, 1997

www.ingramcontent.com/pod-product-compliance
Lightning Source LLC
LaVergne TN
LVHW051847080426
835512LV00018B/3126